COME,
SWEET
DAY

HOLDING ON TO **HOPE** IN DARK TIMES

COME, SWEET DAY

A WRITER'S JOURNEY

JULIANNE DONALDSON

ENSIGN
PEAK

Visit us at shadowmountain.com

ENSIGN PEAK is an imprint of Shadow Mountain Publishing, LLC.

Library of Congress Cataloging-in-Publication Data

Names: Donaldson, Julianne, author.
Title: Come, sweet day : holding on to hope in dark times : a writer's journey / Julianne Donaldson.
Description: [Salt Lake City] : Ensign Peak, [2021] | Includes bibliographical references. | Summary: "Popular fiction writer Julianne Donaldson shares poems that reflect her experiences as a woman of faith to inspire readers to hold onto hope"—Provided by publisher.
Identifiers: LCCN 2020044610 | ISBN 9781629728445 (hardback)
Subjects: LCSH: Hope—Poetry. | LCGFT: Poetry. | Essays.
Classification: LCC PS3604.O5345 C66 2021 | DDC 811/.6—dc23
LC record available at https://lccn.loc.gov/2020044610

Printed in China
RR Donnelley, Dongguan, China

10   9   8   7   6   5   4   3   2   1

For any woman who wonders if what she is
feeling and thinking is unique to her—
others feel that same way and suffer too.

This book was written to remind you that
you're not alone and that there is hope,
even in hard times.

INTRODUCTION

I know every single person out there is dealing with a lot of hard things. But for those who are wondering if they're alone in feeling weighed down by life, you're not. I want you to know that you can be a good person and still have really heavy burdens in this life, and it doesn't mean you're doing anything wrong. You can do everything by the book (and "the book" could be called "How to Have a Successful Life" or "the Bible" or "Relationships 101"), and you can still have earth-shaking losses, grief, and failures. I have learned that nobody is immune to dark times. I have also learned to never take for granted the times when things go well. And I have learned that in order to stretch me, God will allow me to walk through dark times that no amount of hard work, prayer, or faith can prevent.

There have been times in the past few years—times that lasted days and weeks and even months—when I have felt as if the devil had grabbed hold of my feet and was trying to drag me down to the hell of despair. I had a choice. I could look down to where I was going and fall into hopelessness. Or I could call to my God. I could reach up to Him, believing He would grab hold of my hands. And then, with the devil pulling me by the feet and God pulling me by the hands, I would be stretched. Oh, that stretching can be painful. But it's so much better than giving up, looking down, and letting despair claim me.

I am well known as a writer of fiction, but in this book, I share my experiences as a woman of faith. It is my great wish that something I share here will bring you solace, strengthen your faith, and inspire you to hope.

Hold on to hope.
There are good days coming.

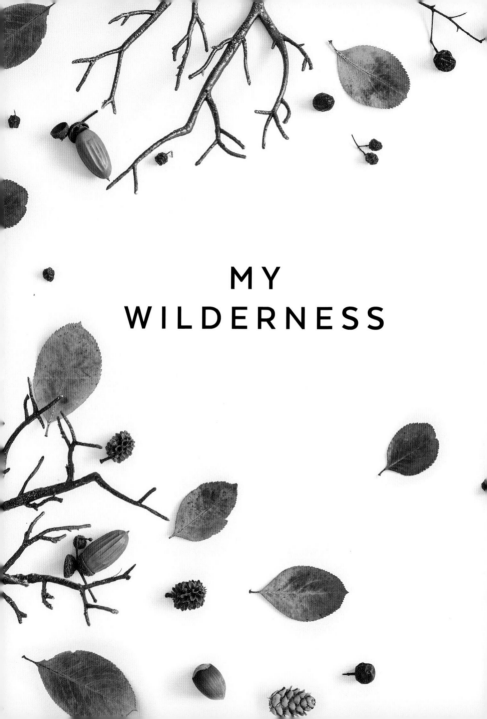

MY
WILDERNESS

A few years ago, my life felt really bleak. My marriage was broken, my career was dying, my debts were mounting, and I felt overwhelmed with the burden of trying to keep everything together for my family. I lay in bed one morning, loath to get out and face another day of crippling stress, and in the quiet stillness between sleep and waking, a thought came to my mind. It came in such purity, I knew it was from God.

The thought was this:

> "For I know the plans I have for you,"
> declares the Lord, "plans to prosper you
> and not to harm you, plans to
> give you *hope* and a future."
>
> —*Jeremiah 29:11, NIV, emphasis added*

The words seared themselves into my heart with the heat of a divine promise. I clung to those words that day. I printed them out and hung them in my kitchen so I could repeat that promise to myself many times a day.

When I received those words, I imagined that my hope and future would look something like a healed marriage, the ability to write under a deadline, and a lifting of the burden of debt. Instead, I was led down a path that included trauma, divorce, long legal battles, mental illnesses, rejection and abandonment, and an inability to write.

Now I hope for a future that looks something like a good man by my side, thriving children, and meaningful work. The other day I stopped in front of that quote and read it again. I wondered when my hope and my future would arrive. And I suddenly had the clearest impression that it had already arrived—that the path I have been led down is part of God's plan for me; this path is not something to be endured until I reach His plan. This *is* His plan!

I have long praised my Lord for delivering me out of captivity, and I recognize that even now, I am following His pattern for delivering His children. He delivered the Israelites out of Egypt, but they still had to cross the Red Sea and wander in the wilderness and starve and be bitten by serpents and wonder if they would ever enter the Promised Land.

This is my wilderness. This is my rough-sea voyage. This is my climb to the top of the mountain to hear the voice of the Lord. This is an essential part of His plan for me. And how do I know that it's essential for my growth? Because if it wasn't, He wouldn't ask it of me. Because if it wasn't, He would spare me this.

God is love, and I can see His love
even in the dark times of life.

Everyone tells me to write

Everyone

Write a sweet story

But I am bitter

Write a love story

But I'm a cynic

Write a funny story

But I grieve

Write to save

Write to laugh

Write to hope

But I am *broken*

Despairing

And unbelieving

Why don't you just *write?*

They ask

I saw their broken hearts

And cried for justice

Envisioned a legion of avenging angels

Fire and brimstone

Lightning bolts and the earth

Gaping open her mouth

To swallow our enemies

"Give me justice!"

I roared to the God of justice

Who sees all

And tolerates no evil

I was answered

By the God of mercy

Who parted heaven's veil

And rained gentleness

Peace

And love

Upon me and mine

A legion of ministering angels

An abundance of goodness

I closed my eyes

Lifted my face to heaven and

Opened my mouth to thank Him

The merciful rain

Washed away the fire and brimstone

Of my heart

And I forgot, for a moment,

Why I cried for justice

No matter how lonely
Or sad
Or hopeless you feel
The world is always turning
Daylight always fades into
Dark night
And if you are lucky
You will glance out
Your kitchen window
While feeling lonely
Or sad
Or hopeless
And see the sky's palette
Of blues

So pristine
So sublime
That you will stop
Washing the dishes
By yourself
And instead stare in awe
And wonder
That a person such as you
Is lucky enough
To live in a world such as this
And the dishes
And the night
And the loneliness
Won't matter so much
Because of the sky

Courage is doing

what you don't want to do

with such kindness

and such a BRIGHT SMILE

that nobody would guess

it was HARD

To all of the families
struggling to
just
get
through
another day:
I'm right here with you.
I have no bragging photos of my kids.
There are no sports teams,
no trophies, no honor rolls.
There are no mission calls,
no dance invitations,
and no vacations.

We don't eat out,
we don't go to movies or sporting
events,
and we don't travel.

What we do is try to survive with
mental illnesses,
trauma,
single parenthood,
and poverty.
We wake up, and if it's a good day,
we all do the work we have to do.

With six of us,
it's very rare
that we all have a good day
on the same day.

And by the grace of God,
this is a life too!

This isn't the first-world life of
accomplishments
and luxury
that I thought I would be living,
but it is a life,
and this—
even this mess—
is worthy of praise.
Even this is worthy of attention.

So, here's me bragging:
I got out of bed today!
We have food to eat.
We are warm.
God is so good to us!

I will keep fighting the good fight.
You keep fighting it too.

At the end of the day,

When your BRIGHT SMILES

Have WORN OFF

And you're just waiting

For your kids to come back to you

And remind you what

Life is all about,

You can sit with the PORCH LIGHT ON,

And that's *courage* too.

Today I didn't write

Today I watched five episodes
Of *Just Add Magic*
With my little boys
Cuddled on the couch
Holding hands with the youngest
During the suspenseful parts

Today I didn't write
Today I walked to a cemetery
And read gravestones
And thought about how precious
Our time is here
With our loved ones
I lay on the grass and sent a message
To an old friend:
Go to Europe with me next year?
Hell yeah was her response

Today I didn't write
Today I made meatloaf
Which is strangely my kids' favorite dinner
Baked potatoes and glazed carrots
We all sat down
Together
Which was also strange
Because usually I'm standing

Tonight I didn't write
Tonight I gave my son a bath
With lots of toys
All the toys
And read books to him in my bed
I let him fall asleep there
With his brother
And the dog
I will sleep somewhere else

This is the only thing I have written today:
That relationships are more important
Than money or success
And that the writing can wait
But living cannot

GRACE

A few years ago, I bicycled every morning. At my best, I was riding twelve miles a day. Then winter came, and the bike went away, and the following summer I was recovering from a major surgery. The summer after that, I was battling the exhaustion that comes with thyroid cancer.

When I pulled my bike out of the garage last week, it had been a full two years since I had ridden regularly. I knew I would be out of shape. But I was astonished at how difficult it was. I was pedaling hard, stopping to walk and stretch my muscles and catch my breath, and getting passed by everyone on the trail. I kept stopping and wondering with embarrassment how I was that out of shape and how I had fallen so far from where I had been before. And why everyone was making it look so easy as they sped past me.

I went home after just a few miles and sat, dejected, in my garage as I considered how far I had to go to return to the state of fitness I had enjoyed just a couple of years before. My teenage son saw me sitting there and asked what was wrong. I told him about my discouraging ride. He got on my bike and rode it down the driveway, then turned around and said, "Both your tires are nearly flat, and you're in a high gear. I couldn't even ride this down the street."

My son pumped up my tires for me and changed the gears. I got back on the bike, and riding was so much easier. Yes, I was still out of shape, but it was nowhere near as hard as it had been just an hour before. I was so relieved.

But here's the thing: I was an experienced cyclist. Why didn't I notice that my tires were flat and my gears too high? Because I was too focused on my own shortcomings.

I thought something was wrong with me because riding was so much harder for me than for others. In reality, something was wrong with my equipment, not with me personally. Sometimes life feels like that. It feels like we're all riding the same trail together and so we must be able to do the same things on that trail. But everyone has a different bike, and some people's bikes have flat tires and are in high gear. My life has felt like that a lot the last few years.

As my family has worked at recovering from trauma, it feels like we're not keeping up with other people. We're falling behind. We're riding hard—as hard as we can—and we're still slow. We're still nowhere near the finish line.

I ask myself often, "What's wrong with me? Why is

this so hard?" But in a gift of grace to myself, I am now telling myself that just because it's hard doesn't mean there's something wrong with me. Just because our progress is slow doesn't mean we're not trying. Just because we have to get off the bike and walk for a while doesn't mean we're failing. And someday, we will be able to put air in our tires and adjust our gears and the ride will be easier.

Until then, I hold on to grace.

My life is spent

Circling altars

Whether kneeling before

Or laid upon

I am never far

From these rough stones

I am never far

From that searing flame

Today I find myself

Laid upon the altar again

I cry a singed-flesh plea

"Lord! Save me!"

He loosens my bands

He takes my place

The sweet-smelling

Smoke of His grace

Rises to heaven

And I—

I am once again

Kneeling before

These rough stones

Whole and unscathed

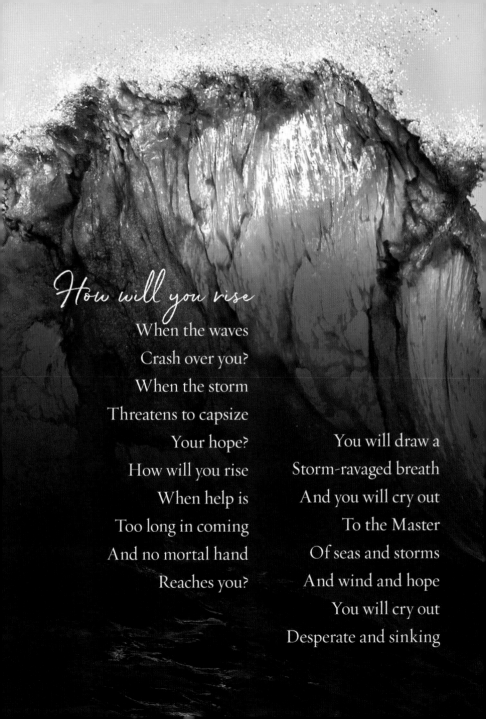

How will you rise

When the waves
Crash over you?
When the storm
Threatens to capsize
Your hope?
How will you rise
When help is
Too long in coming
And no mortal hand
Reaches you?

You will draw a
Storm-ravaged breath
And you will cry out
To the Master
Of seas and storms
And wind and hope
You will cry out
Desperate and sinking

And He will hear you
Instantly
He will reach you
Without delay
He will raise you up
Above the waves
And restore your hope too
This is how
You will rise

I consider my adversary

I count up his debts

That add to my scarcity

I open my mouth to complain

To the Giver of all gifts

And before I can utter the words

I am reminded

"Are we not all debtors?"

I look at my abundance

Of food and health and friends

And close my mouth, silenced

So I count up his offenses

They are many

I open my mouth to complain

To the Holy of all Holies

And before I can utter the words

I am reminded

"Let him who is without sin

Cast the first stone"

I cast my gaze inward

Offenses are sharp but remorse is sharper

I lower my eyes, humbled

And open my hands to let fall

The condemnatory stones

What paradox is this?

I want to hate

Yet I am forced to love

By virtue of my own humanity

And thus the Creator of all that is good

Shows me

The holiness inherent in my fall

And the grace that springs

From the well of my suffering

Everything hangs on Nothing
The mountains
The seas
The sky and sun and stars
The plants and animals and insects
All creatures
Even you and I
Hang
On Nothing
Without Nothing,
There is no point to this
Grand
Awe-inspiring
Majestic
Unfathomable miracle of creation
Without Nothing,
We are limited
We are dust
We are alone
We are lost

Every sacred longing
Of the human heart hinges on
What was found
In that Garden
On that morning
Beyond the stone
Separating life and death
What was found
Was
Nothing
A heaven-and-earth-shaking,
Fall-to-your-knees
Shout-with-wonder
Nothing
And the Nothing found
In the empty tomb
Means
Everything

This is how we lose
Bit by bit
Or all at once
Dreaded
Or surprised
My friend,
We all lose

This is how we grieve
We leave
A group of happy friends
To cry in hiding
Drops and torrents and rivers
Reluctantly
Alarmingly
My friend,
We all grieve

This is how we heal
We sit side by side
In a safe place
With wounds revealed
See the blood still seeping
From yours
And mine

Years have passed
And yet
The well is never dry
My friend,
Tell me why
This well is never dry

If God is in the storm,
Let the wind and hail
Batter me.
If God is in the darkness,
Extinguish the stars,
Banish the moon.
If God is in the climb,
Exile me to the foot
Of earth's highest peaks.
If God is in the deep,
Toss me into
The fathomless sea.
Then make me brave,
Buoy my hope,
And give me faith to endure
This journey to know Him,
Until God is in me.

Every day
Like the widow of Zarephath
I tip the cruse of oil,
Reach my hand
Into the barrel of meal,
Expecting emptiness.
  I am flawed
    Impatient
      Afraid
        Insecure
But I am also His.
And because I am His,
    There is always oil.
      There is always meal.
        Sustenance instead of emptiness
        Deliverance instead of death
        Hope instead of despair

LIGHT

I have never enjoyed shopping. Which means when I'm on a limited budget, like I have been lately, I'm not tempted to buy things because I never go into stores. Generally, I'll just go without. And that is how I went six months without any light in my garage.

Here's the breakdown: One lightbulb burned out. I thought, "Oh well. I can still see." A few months later, another lightbulb burned out. It was dim, but I still had the lights on the automatic garage-door opener. And then one by one, they each burned out until I was left in darkness. Every time I went into my garage, these were my thoughts:

1. It's so dark in here.
2. I don't have any lightbulbs.
3. Even if I did have lightbulbs, the sockets are pretty high up and I don't have a ladder.
4. I don't have time to hunt down a ladder.
5. I don't have money to walk into a store that sells

lightbulbs; I'll be tempted to buy all the things I've been going without.

6. I don't have anyone to help me change the light-bulbs.

7. Man, it's dark in here.

I would either pull out a flashlight or just fumble around in the dark.

A week ago, the sun was out and the snow was melting, and I could feel spring getting ready to make her glorious appearance. So I took an afternoon and cleaned out the garage, which had collected lots of leaves, empty boxes, and other detritus from a busy household. As I was cleaning and organizing, I freed up the space along one wall and suddenly had the very original idea to open the blinds . . . of the window.

I had a window in my garage.

The whole time.

And never once did it occur to me that I could open the blinds.

For six months of darkness, all I could consider was what I didn't have. I didn't have money or time or help. And that whole time, I could have simply noticed what I *did* have. Because what I already had was exactly enough for my needs.

I can't tell you how happy I feel every time I walk into my sunlit garage.

It was so easy to let the light in.
So very, very easy.

In the middle of this gray and cold—

When no sun penetrates the thick haze of

   winter pollution—

I walk outside and hear *birdsong*.

It comes from my neighbor's yard,

Where a grandfather apple tree stretches high

Above the roof of a garage.

I look up to the song

And see small dark birds perched

On skeletal branches against a backdrop of

   drab, bare sky.

The birds peck at apples, dull red,

Hanging like long-forgotten ornaments

Here and there among the branches.

I watch the birds' quick, flitting dance

As they tear flesh from long-ripe fruit

In the death of winter.

And I know what that fruit tastes like.

It tastes like hope.

I am learning to take note
Of the lulls in life
When storms have
Softened their cacophony
And flow
Becomes a sweet normalcy
I take note
This is heaven's breather
This is the quiet
Of uninterrupted sleep
The alarm clock
That didn't need to be set
The children who didn't
Climb into bed with me
This is the luxury
Of waking up
On my own terms
Rested
And happy
I take note
This is tender
This is merciful
This never lasts long
But while it does
I thank God

Tangled in fear,
I spin myself into
A frenzy of worry
Trying to do it all
Until I recall
A different day
A different fear
And a quiet answer
To that day's prayer:
Trust the Giver.

Ah, yes!
Now I remember!
I take a breath
And soften into
The cradle of faith
This is where *peace*
Holds sway

I was dead.

What was once mine

Had been entombed

Sealed up

And abandoned

But then

A sliver of light appeared

It's not real

It's mania

It's delusional

It's pharmaceutical

The crack widened

The light brightened

A quickening happened within

What is this

New life?

How can it be mine

When I was declared

Incapable, broken

And unwanted?

I lift the veil
From over my face
The light is blinding

I leave the tomb
And find myself
In a garden
Now I will find Him
I will bathe His scarred feet
With my tears

And praise Him
The Lord of Resurrection
For raising me up
To a life not at all
Like my old one
But one infinitely more
Glorious

This pale spider

On nimble legs

Spins a web

From filament

So fine

I cannot see it

In this golden

evening light

But can only guess

At its shape

And size

By the movement of

Its architect.

It seems to dance

suspended in

Midair

Working without pause

For its lifesaving

Creation.

It's strange how on this

Sunday evening

Sitting alone on my porch

I am reminded of God

When I watch

This spider

His plans and patterns

Invisible to me

His ways a mystery.

I only know He is

Working industriously

Weaving something

Something beautiful

And lifesaving

For me.

In sunsets
and sunrises
They post painted-cloud
love notes
such as
I know today was hard.
I'm thinking of you.
and
Hold on. There is still beauty to be found.
This sky is a limitless
noticeboard
for such boundless divine love.
Look. There.
Watch Them
gather clouds,
slant sunbeams,
tilt heaven,
and move earth
to prove
how splendidly
and lavishly
They love us.

And still

I wait

Like the robin

In the grass

Feeling the

Pause of life

Alert for the sign

That something

Is coming—

Something good

Hope comes cautiously
In darkness
In winter
In want.
She hushes
The baying dog of old fears
And tiptoes
Through silent rooms
Of loneliness.
She opens doors
That grief had sealed shut.

Hope breathes on
The cold embers of tomorrow
Until a new fire blazes.
She sets a table
Laden with joy
And bids the starved soul
To come and feast
Where she plays the music
The heart most wants to hear.
To the steadfast who wait,
Quietly,
Tenderly,
Courageously,
Hope comes.

HOME

When spring arrived, I bought a bird feeder and two types of birdseed. My kids eagerly helped me assemble the little feeding station outside our family-room window, and then we impatiently waited for visitors.

My four-year-old exercised greater patience staring out that window than he has ever shown for anything else. Day after day, the bird feeder remained empty of visitors and full of seed. I looked outside to see what could be keeping the birds away. Did I not provide a beautiful and sturdy place for them to feast? Did I not give them their favorite food to eat? Did I not chase away the wasps that threatened their habitat? Did I not give them a birdbath as well, full of clean water? What more could I have done?

I lifted my arms to the sky and called out, "Here is all of this for you. For free. We ask nothing of you except to be given the honor of caring for you. We ask for nothing in return. We simply want you to come to our home and feast on what we are offering and let us be charmed by the sight of you. Because we love you."

We waited at the window for days, then held our breath with excitement when a pair of birds, male and female, fluttered to our offering, picked up seeds, then flew away again.

I looked at my children's faces, smiling in innocent joy, reflecting my own feelings. And the lesson is not lost on me. If the Lord feeds the birds in the sky and delights in them the way we do, how much more must He be willing to care for and delight in His own children!

How he rains down blessings upon us, begging us to simply come to His home and feast on what He is offering.

"Come," He calls. "Just come and feast.
I ask for nothing in return.
I simply want you to come home."

This is no relay race.
The Lord
Does not wait at his mark,
Hand stretched back,
Waiting for you
To reach Him.
No.
Against all reason,
He turns away from
The finish line.
He sprints toward you,
Even though it might
Look like the race will be lost
And you are certainly no asset
In partnering with Him.

Nevertheless,

He sprints

Toward you

As you run

Or walk

Or stagger

Or crawl or simply

Cry out

With your face toward Him.

See how

He races to meet you.

See how swiftly He runs

To reach you.

I am recovering from trauma
a living paradox

The more I *heal*
the more I recognize
how broken I am
The more *clarity* I have,
the more I see where
I am still confused.
The *stronger* I become,
the more I realize
how very vulnerable
I am.

And the greater my grief,

the greater my *joy*.
My soul is *expanding*

in both directions

of the human experience.

I would not trade the bitter

if it meant

having to give up the *sweet*.

I would not *give up the joy*

in order to escape the grief.

We all have quiet times
In life
Times of retreat
When we lie prostrate
Because it is all
We can do
I have lived so long
In this quiet time
Life goes on around me
Days stretch into
Months
Then years
Dreams are achieved
And milestones passed
By others
While I lie still
Forehead to the ground
And plead
For my time to stand

I once was a child

Who played possum

At the end of long car rides

For the very real treat

Of being carried

Into the house

By my dad,

My eyes squeezed shut.

He knew I was awake.

He carried me anyway.

Now I have children

That I have carried.

Most of them

Have grown too big

But one is still

Small enough

To hold and lift—

A light, soft body

Nestled against me,

Blonde head

Resting on my shoulder,

Little nose

Pressed against my neck,

A willing abandonment of

"I do it myself!"

For the comfort

And security

Of the carry.

Ah!

The privileges of childhood!

I, too, would give up

All of my

"I do it myself!"

To be carried

Like that

Again.

He is capable
Of such cruelty
He can twist
The strands of fate
Into merciless tragedy
Nothing is assured
Nothing is safe
He gives and
He can take away
There is no permanence
On this earth
And when you know
What He is capable of
You might be
Terrified
Every
Day

Or

When you know

What HE is capable of

You might slip your

Hand into His

And lean on Him.

When you are too

Worn down

With worry and grief

You might ask Him

To carry you

And He will

For He is capable of

That too

And ever willing

Oh, *Spring!*

How I admire you!

You take the snow

That killed last year's life

And drink from it

To bring forth

Not what was old

Not the greens and browns

Of last summer

But riotous and bright

New color

Lacy blossoms

The sweet revival of

Birdsong

The aching blue of your skies

Spring,

You are a wonder!

And you, dear friend

Yes, *you*

You are a wonder too!

When your winter

Is dark and cold

And seems to stretch on

Longer than you can bear

Fill up your reservoirs

Rest and wait

For when your spring comes

You will astonish

And delight us all

With the sublime

And breathtaking beauty

Of your *blooming*

I never knew BIRDS
Began to sing
At 4:15 in the morning
In May.
At 4:15 in the morning
In May
There's no sign
That dawn is coming.
With my human eyes
I can see no evidence
That darkness will
Soon give way
To LIGHT.
But the birds know
Somehow.

These morning greeters
These good-news singers
Even in the dark
They are
Relentlessly HOPEFUL

MERCY

One afternoon I sat in my minivan in the driveway and couldn't stop crying. Something had happened that day with one of my children that broke my heart. I felt devastated, overburdened, and utterly alone in this new trial. After many minutes of trying to stop my tears, I made my way inside and found a package waiting for me. It was from someone I didn't know. She had, months before, seen a post I shared on my Facebook author page and started making a gift for me. It was a beautiful crocheted blanket. I don't know how many weeks or months earlier she had this idea and started this project and finished it and packaged it and mailed it. But it came exactly on time. Exactly. The day when I most needed to know that I was not alone, this tender mercy arrived with the message: You're not alone. God knows you. He is aware of you. I wept even more out of gratitude for this tender mercy.

And then I wrote this poem.

God's mercies,
Thought out
And prepared
Far in advance,
Land so *perfectly*
Into the timeline
Of new heartbreak
That I am caught
And cradled
Mid-crash.
Stunned at the
Perfection of His ways,
I can only weep
Amid tokens
Of His watchful care.
And, oh, how tender
His mercies,
How infinitely tender!

The glory of God
Thrives in extremes.
His light shines brightest
In the deepest cave
The darkest night
The greediest grave.
So I will praise Him
For the evils of this world
For injustice
For want
For injury
For pain
I will praise Him for allowing
Such darkness
That I cannot help but be awed
And saved
By His light.

I have grown accustomed to

QUIET

I have become fluent

in the language of

LETTING GO

Sometimes I forget to inhale

until I am prodded

back to awareness of

Life

and the necessity of breathing

All things change

This, too, is

TEMPORARY

Someday I will

Let go of

QUIET

and stand with

open hands to receive

my next

Divine Gift

One night,
when my burdens
felt overwhelming,
I had a dream
that I walked a tightrope,
arms outstretched,
frozen in fear of falling.
I looked down and saw
stretched below me,
as far as I could see,
a great net.
And standing on the ground,
holding a corner of that net,
was my Lord.
He looked up at me with the
brightest,
easiest,
most joyful smile and said,
"I've got you."
It was His smile that
surprised me most.
Absolute confidence
and happiness at seeing
me.

Me!
Happiness at standing
where I needed Him
and holding my net for me.
It was joyous!
Now every time I feel like
I'm balancing the weight
of my whole family
on my shoulders
and walking the scariest tightrope
that life can offer,
I remember His smile.
I remember His easy and confident words.
"I've got you."

Fill the sails
Rock the waves
Send this boat
To a distant shore
We're on our way to the promised land
And we won't be captives anymore
We're going to the promised land
We're going to the promised land
Across the desert
And the sea
We're on our way, my babes and me

Touch these stones
Light our way
Keep our faces
Turned to Thee
Lead us now to the promised land
O, Lord of our delivery
We're going to the promised land
We're going to the promised land
Milk and honey
Safe and free
We're on our way, my babes and me

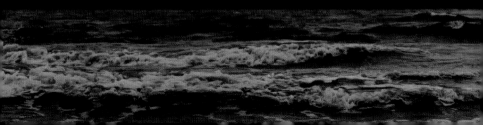

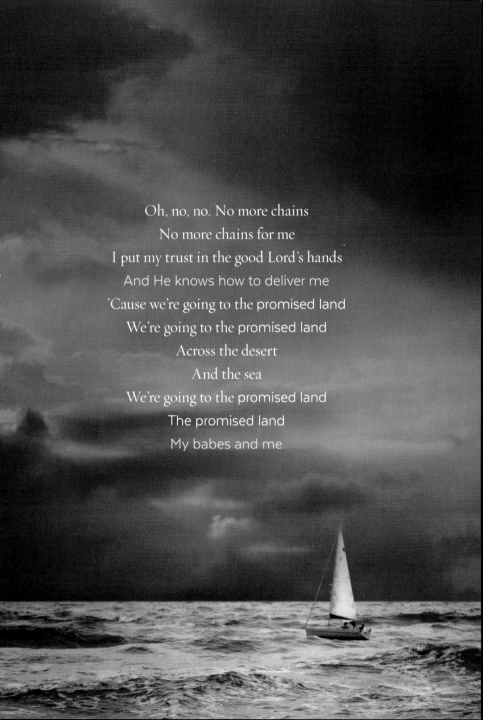

Oh, no, no. No more chains
No more chains for me
I put my trust in the good Lord's hands
And He knows how to deliver me
'Cause we're going to the promised land
We're going to the promised land
Across the desert
And the sea
We're going to the promised land
The promised land
My babes and me

Stand up
O, daughter,
Stand up
Throw off the chains
By which you are bound
Brush off the dust
That place on the ground
Was never meant for you
Daughter,
Come, claim your throne
Come, hold your scepter
Come, wear your crown
Stand up
O, daughter,
Stand up!

If you see me

In my *promised land*

Don't forget my deliverance

Count the steps

I've walked to this shore

And call me

A Red Sea girl

I WILL WAIT FOR YOU

at the end of the world

I will search

this barren wilderness

I will listen for

the *birdsong*

signaling your coming

I will call for you

to come

in the darkness

I will *hope* for you

to come

in my want

I will cry for you

to come

Come, bright hope

Come, new song

COME, SWEET DAY

CONCLUSION

What's so great about the unchosen life? The detours and the derailments and the catastrophes? What's so wonderful about the empty bank account, the broken heart, or the sick loved one?

It's the privilege of seeing the hand of the Lord in your life.

I never knew how much God had prepared for me and how much He works for my benefit until I entered my wilderness—until I started my rough-sea voyage. I had no idea, in my self-sufficiency, how much goodness and generosity live in the hearts of the people all around me. This wilderness I've been living in for the past few years has enabled me to feel more joy and greater love than I ever imagined I could.

What a privilege it is to be chosen for refining! What an honor to be humbled so that I can see Who has been supporting me all along. And how choice are these days when heaven's veil is parted for a moment, and I glimpse angels winging their way to earth to come to my aid.

Healing is a journey. Becoming is a journey. Growth and change are all part of life's test.

For the record, I have not *arrived*. I'm not on the other side of anything. I feel like I've been running a marathon for years now, yet it's only mile thirteen.

For anyone who is just starting their race or feels like it will never end, I'm not on the other side telling you to just keep running. I'm in the pack. With you. Maybe even behind you. And I'm calling out, "Keep running! Keep your head up! This will be worth it! It will all be worth it!" I'm telling it to myself just as much as I'm telling it to you. Because here's the thing: you don't have to get to the other side of a trial in order to be grateful for that trial, or in order to have your faith strengthened, or in order to recognize the compensatory blessings of the Lord.

In fact, if you're thinking you're going to wait until you get to the end to find those things, you'll be missing out. You've got to run the race with your happy shirt on. Run the race because you're grateful to be alive. Run the race because running it will make you stronger than you were before. Run the race because God set the race before you.

God is good. Trust Him.

IMAGE CREDITS

JULIANNE DONALDSON

Julianne Donaldson grew up all over the world as the daughter of a US Air Force fighter pilot. As a result, she has a severe case of wanderlust and frequently dreams of living abroad again. Until her dream is realized, she lives in Utah, where she spends most of her time raising her five children. Her novels *Edenbrooke* and *Blackmoore* have been translated into fifteen different languages and have won numerous awards. This is her first collection of poetry. You can find her online at juliannedonaldson.com.